In the River

Written by Jo Windsor

Jungle rivers
can be long and wide.
Lots of animals live
in jungle rivers.
The animals can get
their food from the rivers.

3

This giant water bug
lives in a jungle river.
It gets fish and frogs
to eat.

This leech lives in the water.
Leeches get blood
from other animals
for their food.

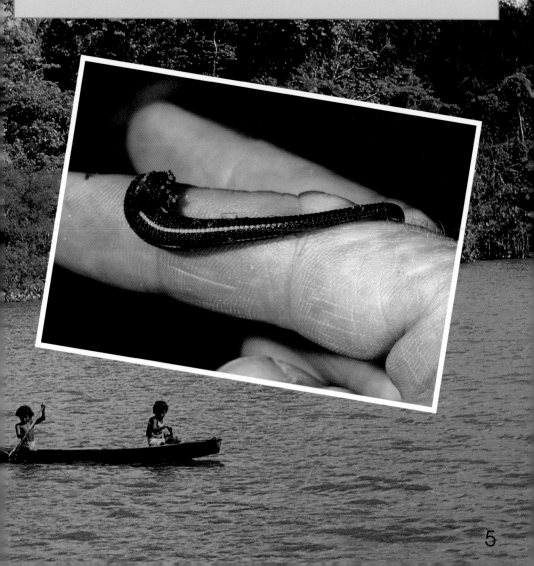

These piranhas live in
a jungle river.
The piranhas can
attack an animal.
They can eat the animal
quickly.

This turtle
lives in a jungle river.
When little fish swim by,
the turtle gets them.
The turtle eats the little fish.

These animals
are called capybaras.
They are like big rats.

They have webbed feet
to help them swim.
They eat plants
from the river for their food.

These animals
live in a jungle river, too.
They are called manatees.

They stay in the water
all the time.
They eat lots and lots
of river plants.

These giant otters swim
in the jungle rivers, too.
They live in groups
and make dens
in the river bank.

Giant otters have webbed feet
to help them swim.
They eat fish and frogs.
They can hold their food
in their paws.

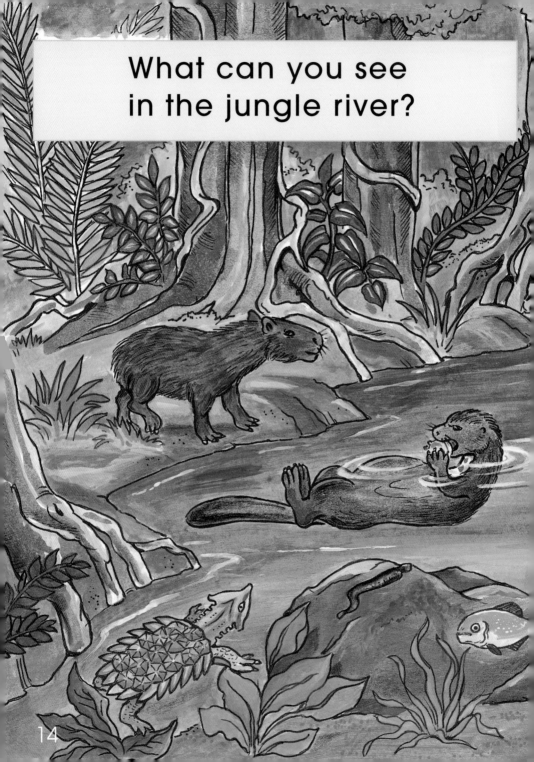

What can you see
in the jungle river?

Index

Guide Notes

Title: In the Jungle River
Stage: Early (4) – Green

Genre: Nonfiction (Expository)
Approach: Guided Reading
Processes: Thinking Critically, Exploring Language, Processing Information
Visual Focus: Photographs (static images), Index

THINKING CRITICALLY
(sample questions)
- What do you think this book is going to tell us?
- What animals do you see on the front cover? Where do you think these animals might like to live?
- Focus the children's attention on the Index. Ask: "What animals are you going to find out about in this book?"
- If you want to find out about a giant water bug, what page would you look on?
- If you want to find out about turtles, what page would you look on?
- Look at page 6. These animals are piranhas. What do you think piranhas like to eat?
- Look at pages 10 and 11. Manatees live in the river. What do you think manatees like to eat?
- Look at page 13. How does the giant otter use its paws when it is eating?
- What do we use when we eat?

EXPLORING LANGUAGE

Terminology
Title, cover, illustrations, photographs, author, illustrator, photographers, title page, index

Vocabulary
Interest words: leeches, piranhas, capybaras, manatees, attack
High-frequency words (new): quickly, their

Print Conventions
Capital letter for sentence beginnings and title, periods, commas, question mark